We're captive on the carousel of time.
We can't return, we can only look
behind, from where we came
and go round and round and round,
in the circle game

- Joni Mitchell The Circle Game

Also by Suzanne Brody

Lunch with Rav Dimi 2021
Mermaid Tears 2020

UNEARTHED

by

Suzanne Brody

720 Sixth Street, Unit #5
New Westminster, BC
V3L 3C5
CANADA

Title: Unearthed
Author: Suzanne Brody
Publisher: Silver Bow Publishing
Cover Art: "Nevada Sunset" painting by Candice James
Cover Layout and Design: Candice James
Editing: Candice James

All rights reserved including the right to reproduce or translate this book or any portions thereof, in any form without the permission of the publisher. Except for the use of short passages for review purposes, no part of this book may be reproduced, in part or in whole, or transmitted in any form or by any means, either by means electronically or mechanically, including photocopying, recording, or any information or storage retrieval system without prior permission in writing from the publisher or a licence from the Canadian Copyright Collective Agency (Access Copyright).

www.silverbowpublishing.com
info@silverbowpublishing.com
ISBN: 978-1-77403-205-3 paperback
ISBN: 978-1-77403-106-0 electronic book
© Silver Bow Publishing 2022

Library and Archives Canada Cataloguing in Publication

Title: Unearthed / by Suzanne Brody.
Names: Brody, Suzanne, 1976- author.
Description: Poems.
Identifiers: Canadiana (print) 20220158479 | Canadiana (ebook) 20220158487 | ISBN 9781774032053
   (softcover) | ISBN 9781774032060 (HTML)
Classification: LCC PS3602.R64 U54 2022 | DDC 811/.6—dc23

In memory of Mr. Harris (1926-1993), a teacher who made a real difference and was the first to see and comment on many of these poems

And for my children, who are now as old as I was when I wrote these

Unearthed

Introduction

I was a prolific writer in my teen years, jotting down poems on napkins, scrap paper, or even the back of my dad's old business cards. At some point, I acquired mini notebooks that I carried everywhere (as evidenced by their current very beaten-up state) and eventually even began keeping a regular hard-cover, bound journal. All of these as well as my school notebooks and assignments were carefully tucked away in my childhood bedroom after college when I moved out of my parents' house and across the country. On recent trips to visit my parents, I rediscovered this treasure trove that captures my teenage thoughts and feelings. With only some minor editing, I found that this collection resonates both with my adult self and with my own teenage children.

Unearthed

Contents

Tribute ... 13
Mr. Harris ... 14
Writer's Block ... 15
Messages ... 16
Capturing the Moment ... 17
Atlas ... 18
Driving to L.A. ,,, 19
Moving ... 20
The Ghost ... 21
Summer Innocence ... 22
Night Writer ... 231
Someday ... 24
29 February 1993 ... 25
Class Dreams ... 26
Camouflage ... 27
Hold On ... 28
Uneven Exchange ... 29
The Sorrow Inside ... 31
Graduation Season ... 32
Safam Concert ... 33
A World of My Imagination ... 34
Mrs. Saval ... 35
Tuesday Morning ... 36
Security ... 37
Camp ... 38
Another Hot Morning ... 39
Signs of Early Spring ... 40
Hanging Up ... 41
Heeded Advice ...42
Unfamiliar Quotes ... 43
Sticks and Stones ... 44
Playspace Entertainment ...45
All of Us ... 46
Cast Recording ... 47
Peter Pan ... 48
Gratitude ... 49

Trees ... 50
Searching ... 51
Pendulum ... 52
Lost ... 53
Simple Treasures ... 54
Boxing the Demon ... 55
Pain ... 5657
Self Protection ...
Background to a Conversation ... 58
Eclipse of the Moon ... 60
Missing Pieces ... 61
Disappearing Trick ... 62
Singing Zebra ... 63
13 June ... 64
Another Battle ... 65
Dating Revelations ... 66
Bust Trip ... 67
Auld Lang Syne ... 68
Coming Home ... 69
O.K. ... 70
Nursery Nonsense ... 71
Coloring ... 72
Ode ... 73
Roller Coaster ... 74
(Caged) Butterfly ... 75
Goals ... 76
After the Storm ... 77
Brainless ... 78
Remember ... 79
Someone Special ... 80
Breakfast in Newtonville ... 81
Not an Afternoon Special ... 82
Mission ... 83
Phoenix ... 84
The Importance of Place ... 85
In My DNA ... 86
A Watched Pot ... 87
Nostalgia ... 88
Living Ghost ... 89

Pep Talk ... 90
Inner Earthquake ... 91
Collage ... 92
At Peace ... 93
New Driver ... 94
View from the Tayelet ... 95
Distorted Image ... 96
Colorful Crime ... 97
Goodbye ... 98
Aftertaste ... 99
Mothers/Children ... 100
Wounds ... 101
Waiting ... 102
Fear ... 103
Vanilla Confusion ... 104
Eulogy for a Bridge Player ... 105
Blanket Cave Moments ... 106
Healing ... 107
Peaceful View ... 108

Unearthed

Tribute
In memory of Mr Harris

He taught: Simplify.

His gruff voice dissected books,
bespoke dry humor, concealed softness.

A taskmaster, he made us strive for perfection;
rewarded us with chalk missiles and inverted checks.

He animated words, gave us the gift of literature
and a ten-cent pen, lined paper and a voice of our own.

With flannel shirts and stockinged feet
he perched on flimsy desks, ruled the class
and won my loving respect.

Mr. Harris

The tears come
only after numbness
has dulled the vacuum
of an empty spot here.

I see his toe
peering out from a sock
freed from a shoe of convention.

A flannel shirt
masks gravelly voice
discussing grammar or literature
and a friendly harassment
of a slow learner.

He made the mouse an eggshell
and me the voice of Holden,
opened my eyes to plays
and forced me to achieve.

He will always be
in the spirit of my pen.

Writer's Block

I have this boiling,
bubbling of ideas
festering
in the chill night air.

But, inside
they drip away
like blood
leaving my body
empty and unfulfilled.

Messages

Yesterday's laughter
still rings in my ears
and lingers into tomorrow.

My tears and anger
evaporate,
disappearing like clouds
chased away by the sunshine
of your voice.

In the silence
can you hear
the beating of my heart
and the messages it sends?

Capturing the Moment

Paint a picture with words
to adorn a cake
ablaze with the flames
of years gone by.

Color the voices bright
so they can be heard whispering
without a hearing aid.

Scent it with cosmetics
sprinkled with the dust of age
and clothing fighting mothballs.

Dress the heroine in faded skirts
hidden by an apron, topped with a hat
and embraced by a sweater.

Draw the telephone busy
caught in a web of details
while the car sits patiently
waiting to creep on errands.

Paint a picture with words,
but don't forget
to wrap it with a kiss.

Atlas

The weight of the earth
fragilely perched
on narrow shoulders,
breaking a back
and slowly sinking -
creating a hole in space.

A sweat-streaked face
gallantly trying
to withstand the pressure
and hold the universe together.

A shrug of the shoulders,
convulsion of muscle
causing the continents to rattle.
No one would dare deliberately drop
this precious bundle of life...
but what if it's the only way out?

Somewhere in space
a reverberating sigh of relief
and anguished cries echo
as aching shoulders
are relieved of their burden.

Driving to L.A.

From the tiny red car
speeding through endless fields
her laughter flies
over corn and hay
across the dirt road
where a boy waits
beside his dusty mare.

Roof down, music up,
the young couple
whizzes to a new life.

Puffing along the same vast stretches,
stopping at every roadside diner,
resting eyes and dripping forkfuls of pie,
the seasoned driver
of a beat-up company eight-wheeler
follows slowly
into the smog-filled city.

Moving

We moved away, at least in miles,
but sometimes my memories
seem more real than life.

We come back sometimes
just to drive by our old house
and remember.

Invited inside,
I visit someplace foreign
in my own old home.

The kitchen -
unrecognizable, almost.
The dining room
looked like a stranger's.

Worst of all was the bathroom
where everything was the same
except the towels and toothbrushes.

Thank goodness we didn't go upstairs;
seeing my yesterday room transformed
would be unbearable, worse ...
than when I couldn't remember
what it looked like.

Now it's a stranger's house
that belongs to me
only in memories.

The Ghost

Haunting, beckoning,
teasing with old memories.

A hollow shell
of friendships
that are no more.

Mysteriously
opening a door
where faces I once knew
lead me down an old path ...
laughter, crying, and confusion
falling down on me
like snow.

Once more the memory ghost calls,
motions me to follow
through a maze of memories.

I follow with bittersweet ease.

Summer Innocence

The light of a star hanging
on the crescent of a silver moon,
swinging softly like the hammock
whispering on the twilight porch.

A little girl in a frilled night dress
peers out the screen and watches
her fiery clock chime bedtime
under a curtain of mist on the teddy bear
left outside to swing through supper,
to bathe in the night air
while she filled the tub with soap
and blew dry baby curls
as a warm wind
continued to rock the bear
and blow out the sun.

Night Writer

In a pitch-black room
an open window
funnels a silver beam.

Piercing the darkness
it illuminates a piece of paper.
Swiftly, silently scratching,
a pen moves across the page.

Shadow for a face
bent over the single ray,
capturing a moment.

Forever.

Nothing else stirs
as a figure rises
leaving an offering
to a Moonbeam.

Someday?

I'm scared.

What I want is easy...
how many times
have we joked
and said someday...?

But someday was far away,
a safe distance in a place
where real issues never intrude.

When a vision nears reality,
ugly monsters rear heads of complications
and my gut twists and turns.

Today?
Time to face the fear
to realize the dream.

29 February 1993

Remember
fourteen months ago,
a darkened theater
and a question answered
by a flippant smile?

Today
not squeezed
between yesterday
and tomorrow,
a brief release
from the pressured world;
when will we celebrate?

Dirtied drifts
still cover the frozen ground,
and our noses drip
into quilted paper;
but we're immune
from winter colds.

Class Dreams

Behind the clicks and scratches
of marks pressed into lines
to externalize memory,
the fading buzz of a teacher
gives way to impossible snapshots
of perfect familial harmony
and a tangle of arms warmly-tanned
in the sun of roses and May.

The noises of tilting chairs righting
returns the gaze to the interminable present
and the black wand
that takes lifetimes
to point to the next number.

Camouflage

Scribble, doodle, twirl the pen.
Color, write, look busy.

Don't let them know.
They'll never guess,
how you really feel.

Appear engrossed in some activity,
so they never think
you want to be included
in their smiling conversation
even if there is nothing to talk about.

Just continue to
scribble, doodle, twirl the pen.
Color, write, look busy;
but never ever let them know
you're lonely.

Hold On

Her words of advice
echo through my head,
fitting the situation
better than anyone
could have predicted.

Hold on.
I know her every syllable
was scripted by another
for a scene
vastly different from my life;
yet it seems
she looks into my eyes
and reads my code of pain.

I listen to her singing,
'hold on',
and silently reply to myself,
I'll do as she suggests.

Uneven Exchange

Have you not learned yet
the power of words?
The way in which they work
to build or break -
and yours have done the latter.

You tell me what I do
is not meant for a lady
and my bag weighted with books
you melt with a scornful eye,
even knowing this is the world
I built for myself.
You scorn the energies
I pour into battered texts
and the memorizing of words
that were yours from birth
in a language
where not even the alphabet
is something I can claim as my own
without effort.

You say
I can never hope to understand
the world you're from,
yet I forgive the crusted opinions
you have offered me.
In your sorrow
at being far from home
in an alien country
my arms are there to comfort you
and I take away from my time
to fill yours.

Across the darkness,
I share my thoughts,
listening to the stories of your heart -
still you refuse to call me friend.

But when I run from the room
I do it to protect you
from the hurt
that boils inside me
threatening to explode.

The Sorrow Inside

A weak crease of the lips
upturned at a joke
hiding the sorrow inside.

The eyes don't laugh.

Graduation Season

It's ice cream weather,
the sunny green coaxing thoughts
between the panes of frost
to an imperceptible stirring.

But for me it's flood season
as salty rivers control me,
overflow for invisible reasons,
hide from restless sandals
anxious to chase frisbees.

In these t-shirt days
I'm collecting flimsy stuffing moments
to fill a teddy bear
to assail the approaching days
blasting cold air:
pumping it through the aorta,
killing the flowers,
coloring the lawn.

Safam Concert

The songs of my people
soothe my insignificant problems
as I become a timeless voice
repeating ancient words
with my ancestor's intonation.

I unite with these strangers who are kin,
who share my past,
our hearts holding the same longing
to return home -
to a place we've never been.

Tears press my eyes,
relieving years of collective oppressions,
renewing the bonds
to which I pledged myself
in devoted study,
and they float out
to join the songs.

A World of My Imagination

Rainbow trees
of jumping frogs
splashing the air
in a splatter paint
of graffitied walls.

A new world
of jumbled wallpaper
and hidden sounds
where nothing exists.

Mrs. Saval

Today I dress in black
hoping to feel saddened
by this loss;
but just like any other day
she did not cross my mind unprompted.

Then, with a moment of focus,
one single tear
splashed from my eye.

I thought of a neighbor
as she stood on her porch,
recalled her house
and the many times
I darted inside and out
gathering poppy seed cookies;
remembering
the kind woman
who will bake them no more.

Tuesday Morning

The dawn wakes over the window sill
whispering a message of morning
moments before a raucous alarm.

A figure mixes milk and cereal -
the energy for a too-long morning.

Moments later a car purrs to life,
speeding the driver towards the day
and the massive structure
where lessons mingle with friends.

The dying motor hurries the passenger
into a room damp with chlorine,
where pristine water is sliced apart
twenty times by each damp body
before it is left in silence
for the chatter of showers,
the ring of the bell,
and the monotony of another day.

Security

It's a blanket
wrapping around you,
a chair or bed
molding to your shape,
a pair of old shoes
to slip into,
a great big hug
engulfing you inside,
returning home
to warmth and comfort.

It's a sense of belonging
of being smothered
in love and caring
and familiarity;
being safe,
knowing who you are.

Camp

Returning,
so, it seems,
as if we never left.

A sense of belonging,
of being home,
pervades the air
as we wait in line
again
to keep the lice out.

Everyone is older
with more stories
and memories to share,
yet it's all the same
even if
different people share my bunk.

I have come back
to my second home
for the last
memorable time.

Another Hot Morning

Ice cream mixes with sweat
on the dirt of toddlers' palms,
parents cower under umbrellas
of green leafy branches,
children's legs
melt into slides
and the ice cream man
is the king of the castle.

A frustrated gardener
makes futile attempts
to revive dead grass
while on the peeling porch
two grey-haired ladies
rock before a fan
recalling worse heatwaves
but no one listens anymore.

Signs of Early Spring

The grass repopulates the lawns,
children shed bulky jackets
and momentos of gardens grow on clothing.

The winter's dust is swept out of houses,
people wake up to the calls of birds,
and it's still light outside at supper time
as the grill gets cleaned.

Hanging Up

A tenuous cord of thin wire
stretches across the distance,
a small link
holding us together.
In my ear
his voice reverberates
and I imagine
he is beside me.

Reluctant to let go,
I chatter and joke
in an effort to sustain this brief contact.

But we fall silent
as inwardly I struggle
to say three words,
eight simple letters
so obvious and fragile.

My courage failing,
I whisper a substitute...
and hear a soft click.

Knowing we will speak again,
still I fear the power
of the broken connection.

Heeded Advice

The Talmud's wisdom,
for centuries preserved,
taught to youngsters
and debated
in endless arguments.

Laws spanning time,
words of the sages,
true and ageless.

The Talmud teaches
to choose a friend
and I have listened
to its ancient voice.

I have chosen you.

Unfamiliar Quotes

Reaching out
they grab me,
mutant meanings
of familiar quotes.
Distorted messages
speaking just to me
in a riddle
only I can interpret.

Shivers run my spine
as rivulets
wet my face.
Comforting words
heard so often
now twisted and tangled
into near-menacing shapes.

Sticks and Stones

I let the music swirl
filling the air and my soul
with words
in a sacred tongue.
The soothing tones
wash away the hurt.

Dirty Jew …
a stain to be proud of.

A pain that heals
into stronger people
worthy
to speak ancient words
and have a special tie
to millions of people,
thousands of years,
volumes of history
and joyful song
that cleanses my room.

Playspace Entertainment

I am the Pied Piper
luring
with balls of dancing color
that float from my magic wand;
holding spellbound
the children clustered near,
eager to follow
my potion of soap and water,
the raindrop pearls
that burst with joy
on outstretched fingertips.

All of Us

When all of us were younger,
we were protected from the world.

All of us
were friends,
but now we're each alone
with different crowds of people.

One of us
overdosed on drugs
and now lives in rehabilitation.
One of us
tried suicide
and his fate lies
undecided in a hospital bed.
One of us
has a talent
for which she won a prize.
One of us
lives a life of average.
One of us
ran away from home
and has yet to be found.

All of us
have taken different paths
and chosen things
the others did not choose.

And I wonder ...
what will become of us.

Cast Recording

Waves of sound
wash over me
like a gentle lapping
of warm water.
Familiar words
cling close
like damp clothes
tracing my body.

My mind takes flight
on wings of fancy
anticipating what is to come
as the music swirls
to create a picture
before my eyes.

I see the action
as if I were in the audience
once more at the theater
and I let the songs
sweep me away.

Peter Pan

I am Peter Pan
'cause I don't wanna grow up.
But everyone around me
is transforming,
growing into
people I don't recognize
with interests I don't share ...

So I fly with Tinkerbell
off to Never-Never-Land.

Gratitude

Thank you
for being an ear
when I was a voice box,
for being silence
when I was shouting,
for leading me
to new ideas
and for being an example
of whom I strive to be.

For not requesting
more than I'm ready to give,
and just for being you,

Thank you.

Trees

A sea of green
waves of leaves, life
silence punctuated
by a hazel house
with Gables peering,
a lifeboat above the sea.

Behind this landmark
a lone individual
red, orange - different
among the waves of conformity.

Searching

They travel in packs
painted and dolled up
talking loudly.
They display themselves
revealing
a little cleavage or leg
like hooks, fishing
trying to catch a man.

I travel alone,
walking softly,
letting little pieces of soul
serve as bait,
but no one is biting.

It seems no-one
is searching for a best friend.

Pendulum

A pendulum
swings inside my head
deciding the outcome
of an inner debate –

yes,
       no,
              yes,
       no
              and back
again.

I'm getting dizzy
following this never-ending indecision
and wish the pendulum
would settle in one spot,
    yes or no.

Suspended inside myself,
I stand precariously
on the swinging object
that may decide my future.

Wildly wavering
the pendulum still will not rest.

Lost

Where do you go
when every step
is a wrong one,
and a foot finds a mouth?

An appropriate spot?

What can eyes
blinded by tears,
stuck in a tunnel,
see of the world around?

How does anyone
          recover
from wounds of the soul?

Simple Treasures
- For S.G.

Thank you
for holding my hand,
giving me your shoulder,
and holding me together.
You were there to listen
when the grief tumbled out
with nagging questions,
a torrent of emotions.

And when the words choked me
you were there
to muffle the tears
or join in the smiles,
weak and strong.
Thank you
for helping me along
a rough ride without a floor,
for being there
when the laughter returned.

For those who stood there
blindly concerned
without an explanation
thank you for the hands
you held out to help me up
when an invisible rock
sent me sprawling.

My ear, shoulder, hands, and arms
will be there for you
as yours were
for me.

Boxing the Demon

When will the demon
leave me alone?

I box with his shadow
and it has your face
unstained by tears,
not mauled
by my futile blows.

Don' t you realize
I can't lose this fight?

Pain

A searing pain
through my inner gut
looks to others
like reddened eyes
and swollen nose
caused by the tears
they never see spill
in torrents
from an aching heart.

Stone walls
and transient smiles
cannot chase the pain away.

So I try learning
to walk doubled over
to contain the leaking.

Self-Protection

An invisible barrier
holds the world at bay,
letting pass
only the privileged few.

My conversations
bloat with hidden meaning
telling pieces of the story
to those skilled
in the art of listening,
decoding,
joining me
in unnecessary subtle subterfuge.

My world feels laced
with unseen menace.

Background to a Conversation
An explanation to K.P.M.

It ended much the way it began
but the intervening years
gave the story a different twist,
a new life with altered casting
and unexpected aftermath.

The tentative inevitability
with which our lives
twined themselves together
grew, blossomed, and thrived
amidst the transitions of life
and transient outside tensions.

An end was unthinkable,
Unimaginable
and suddenly
quite real
in a drawn-out drama
that left me daily in limbo
with no one for support.

For the months of darkness
tears, brooding, bleakness
and lack of appetite.

I have no words
to capture a feeling
of living in a cage,
a life not my own.

But you who have traveled
the same dark forest

of the soul and mind
will read between the lines
until you reach
a little blue pill
that brings a ray of light
but cannot fully vanquish
the monsters
lurking behind the trees.

Eclipse (of the moon)

We circle round each other
doing the mating dance of swans
as slowly you approach me
oblivious to the million twinkling eyes
and hundred glittery lenses
watching.

You are the vibrant, fiery one
I the lonely pile of rocks
eagerly seeking your warmth.

Slowly I begin to lose myself
in the shadow of your light.
Willingly and unknowingly
submitting myself to you,
becoming a second image of yourself.

By the time I realize
it is too late to struggle free
a single blackness
is all the diamonds see.

Missing Pieces?

I am the caulk
to fill the cracks in your life;
the instrument
you deign to air
until my endless lyric chatter
gives you a headache
and I am banished
to the shadowed corner.

I am the patch
to cover up spare time
and hide
the holes in your life.

I am the equal of nothing,
friend of the invisible,
not the world to you,
though you are that
without which I am incomplete.

You do not need
another drop of life
to fill a heart
or provide a reason to rejoice.

But I think
I do.

Disappearing Trick

I feel myself
splitting at the seams,
crumbling
into little bits
of dust.

The sure-footed mountain goat
has been replaced
by a broken tea kettle
that can no longer
cry for relief.

I am melting;
a pile of salty water
that will soon
cease to exist.

Singing Zebra

Dancing hands
create a waterfall
cascading over rocks,
zebra's free to play
to a unicorn's medley.

Bobbing keys,
a babble of voices
beneath strong guidance
fly free
in a black box.

13 June

Two skins
like ice cream
melted together,
one indistinguishable
from the other…

Curiosity pulsing,
emboldening fingers
provoking exploration…

Breathing punctuates
the day turned night,
highlights awareness
and I never want
to take my own skin back.

Another Battle

A swordfight of tongues
and always
I must lick my wounds
as with every cell
I strive to leave a scar,
strike out on my own,
leave her overbearing wing.

But I am only
flighting myself.

Dating Revelations

I never knew a hand
could melt a body's soul
with the slightest
whisper of a touch,
electricity could spark
with just a caress.

The spiderweb you traced
in the lines of my palm
and the warmth radiating
from the gentle enclosure
of your hand
gently creeping across mine
in the darkness of a theater
where eyes did not see
and ears barely heard
because all that mattered
were palms and fingers
dancing to the beat
of a single drummer.

Bus Trip

My companions
are black squiggles
in straight lines
filling a white page
of silent thoughts
running in circles
inside my head.

We are carried forward
isolated
from the buildings
full of lives
we pass
at a steady
slightly swaying,
bumpy rate
for hours
of deadening immobility.

Auld Lang Syne

Like schoolchildren
waiting for the bell
clanging freedom and fresh air
they hold champagne glasses
and slow the clock
with incessant stares
and as the two black hands
meet at the top,
whistles and cheers erupt.

Coming Home

Like gold filigree
lights adorn the night
and weave a tapestry
carelessly flung
upon ebony floor.

We gradually circle,
wafting lower
as the eagle
coming home to nest.

We stiffly stand,
filing like ants
through narrow aisles
until hidden grains of sand
fall from creased jeans
and are buried in the snow.

O.K.
-   To 7 July

A drop of sand
in the pool of words,
but it created
the pearl
I discover anew each time.

You'd think by now
I could trace your features,
etch them in my dreams,
yet every time
unexplored regions
quiver under my fingertips.

Familiar routines,
time-worn phrases
and you are embedded
in my very soul,
so secrets melt
like Dorothy's witch
splashing me
with a scent of you.

Nursery Nonsense

Blue and green of winter dawn
standing in a snow cake.
I am winter,
you are dawn,
our baby is a little boy
riding on a dragon's wings,
catching clouds
and chasing rabbits
through a dandelion brier.

Purple and pink
of summer snow
that lights on noses
and melts on tongues,
finding the kitten's lost mittens.

Cold air blows in,
around and under
a mossy cottage
in hidden dell
beneath a lion's paw.
We float in foam
upon the moon
until the book is closed,
stopping the snail
on its way to work.

I am dawn
and you are winter,
our baby is a little girl
who hugs you close
to kiss goodnight.

Coloring

The waxy smell
of a rainbow
scattered, jumbled,
spilling over
the blank page
waiting to receive life.

One by one,
filling in lines,
animating shapes.

A child proud
of creating a universe
breathes in the wax
and wears the rainbow
down to colored teardrops.

Ode

Perfect half moons
falling from the sky
onto a bed of tissue-cloud
at a clip of thunder.

Hands shorn
of protective daggers,
toes defeated
by metal jaws
ominously snipping.

Rain drips
onto the scattered
crescents of epidermis
which lie in waste,
forever parted
from the nurturing being
that gave them life.

Roller Coaster

It's a never-ending
roller coaster,
taking me
for a ride.

Sometimes
I want
nothing more
than to get off;
other times
I hope it never ends.

Powerless,
on the ups and downs
and loop-de-loops
my white-knuckled grip.

The clearest proof
I'm on this ride of my life
until the end.

(Caged) Butterfly

I envy you
for the butterfly you are
free to wander
among the sweetest gardens
while I remain
locked behind these walls.

I want to join you,
to flitter between the flowers,
but I beat my wings
against restricting bars.

Will you join me here
in the cramped space of my world,
wait with me
until the day
my door opens?

Goals

Set your goals too high
and you fall;
reaching
for the impossible
makes for disappointment.

Set your goals too low
and you never know
all the accomplishments
you let pass you by.

Set your goals just right
so you stretch
just a little more
until you arrive.

But no one can tell me
which describes the goal
I set myself to pursue.

After the Storm

The rainbow falls
dropping into pearls
of summer dew
and winter snowflakes
gilding the edge
of a butterfly wing.

Sizzling color
crying confusion,
dancing with the naked wind
and spiraling up
to kiss the cloud
raining sparkling teardrops
and weaving
invisible spider trails
catching the sun.

The daisy watches
and, dazzled,
hides herself
in pieces of broken rainbow.

Brainless

My brain is mush
of that I'm sure.
I could not tell you more.
the problem,
you see,
is not you or me.
it's my brain I'm afraid
that's gone berserk.
No need to worry,
simply a quirk.

My control center
is on the blink
and I'm in the pink.

All that this proves
is I'm insane
but causing no pain.

Yes it's true
that for a thinker
all I have
is a blinker.

Sometimes I'm there,
other times not.
No need to worry
for I'm fine,
right as rain,
just missing a brain.

Remember

Zachor
Remember,
the flaming word proclaims.
Remember
the destruction
of the Temples
and remember
the pain and suffering
of the Holocaust.

Blazing across the sky
a single word
simple in meaning
yet conveying so much.

The fire now ashes
engulfed by black sky
but still burning
behind my eyes
and I remember.

Someone Special

You're someone special
who brings laughter and smiles,
unknowingly teaching me,
making my life
a brighter place to live.

You're someone special
who shares my interests
and is capable
of making the world eximious.

You're someone special
and there is no gift
I can tie with a bow
that will show you
what you mean to me.

So, I hope you'll accept
my words instead.

Breakfast in Newtonville

A hasty muffin
sheds a trail along crusted jeans
and ripped books
stuffed with wrinkled grades -
the frustrated works
of a genius undiscovered.

Uncombed hair ties knots
beneath a once-white baseball cap
as last night's dirt is scrubbed away
and the lukewarm coffee
chases away the taste of sleep and beer.

Muffin bits fall to the tiled floor
as cup and napkin are thrown
three points
a glum reminder of younger days
in a yellow kitchen and rainbow classroom.

The tired bag hiked upon a shoulder,
the burden of another day
begins as dusty boots
trudge their way to school.

Not an Afterschool Special

Two short paragraphs
hidden on page seven,
a panicked phone call
leading to confirmation.

In elementary school
we played together
on swings and jungle gym
and I never knew…
a year later in critical condition
from an overdose of his grandpa's pills.

They pumped his stomach
and he was lucky.
She was not.
No newspaper story to warn me,
just an empty seat in every class
and a whispered rumor of slit wrists
or was it hanging?

Depended on who told it.
Didn't matter,
her seat was still empty
like in those movies
on tv after school,
but those shows never told me
how it really felt
to know the faces
of those of us dying
too young to live.

Mission

This is the land
of prayers and history
but my eyes are dry
and my heart silent
while within others
mountains are moved.

They applaud fate
for bringing them here
at the right time
with the perfect group
but I still question
the choices I made
and the wisdom
of being here now.

Phoenix

The phoenix
rises triumphant
from a bed of ashes,
like the flowers of spring,
pushing aside deadened ground.

A city is built
from ancient ruins
and the sun greets
new life slowly grown
out of another's death.

I am becoming
a phoenix, too.

The Importance of Place

The questions, issues
raised in a place
out of time
fester in a mind
not used to exercising them,
not able to provide
the outlet they demand.

There, the ideas grew,
floated in the air,
were caught in conversation,
permeated the atmosphere.

Here the air is devoid
of gentle whispers.

Questions begging answers
and ideas
are slowly suffocated.

In My DNA

The sound of the songs
watched by two flickering lights
and a Friday night
flavored with the smell of challah
eaten still warm from the oven.

The joyous dance in a circle
spotlighting the heavy scroll
as we move
to popular music
not played on mainstream radio.

The holidays
that divide my calendar
into lunar months
and make my mouth water
for particular tastes.

The foods forbidden
to cross the threshold
where one set of dishes
lies unused 51 weeks a year.

A history preserved in stories
connecting us
through time and space.

A Watched Pot

I sit here
eyes soaked in redness
cheeks and nose
resembling rivers,
a silent machine
docile at my side.

I know I have
no big crisis
over which to moan,
but I wish this quiet
would be broken
by your voice
instead of just the striking clock,
so I continue
watering my room.

Nostalgia

Remember
when there were good guys and bad guys?
And the good guys always won
Somehow?

How we were never tired
even when we yawned
and nine o'clock
was late at night?

The stories we made up
before we really knew
what printed letters said?

When we had time
to laugh and play and color
and a fight was over
as soon as it began?

Now the bad guys often win.
Nine o'clock is afternoon.
We are buried under books and papers
and grudges last forever.

The adults had all the answers.

Now we discover
there are only questions.

Living Ghost

As I walk through the halls
peering into classrooms,
surveying your one-time haunts,
with the sound of a footstep
I startle and search the crowd
thinking you'll be there.

Out of the corner of my eye
I scan the busy halls
for a glimpse of you.

Old habits die hard
even though I know
you have moved on.

Pep Talk

Go for it
used to be so easy,
set a goal
and soar past,
confident
the world was mine.

Now doubts,
tricky choices
and goals just out of reach;
do I dare try?

Inner Earthquake

I've built myself
a fragile world
of building blocks
precariously stacked,
swaying in an attempt
to touch the sky.

You are the foundation,
the cornerstone
upon which everything rests.

And I realize
as you walk away
and a thunderous clap
precedes the ruins of a civilization,
these wooden blocks were nothing
but dreams and plans.

No one will blame you
for the collapse,
not even I,
knowing the restacked pieces
will be a little wetter
maybe dented
and slightly rearranged.

Collage

Snapshots
capturing moments
of you, of me, of us...
scrap paper and napkins
filled with quotes,
a secret phone number,
mementos of card games and bus rides
and time shared
around so many different tables.

Hallway meetings,
notes passed between classes,
favorite quotes,
words in many tongues,
programs from so many concerts and shows
and now... nothing new to add.

At Peace

In the absence of light
soft whispers of thoughts
understood without words
encircled by arms
leaning one upon the other
and needing nothing more.

Supporting each other
when in the darkness
one starts to fall,
they sit wrapped in a blanket
made of their own little world
illuminated from within.

New Driver

Watching the world
fly past the windows,
white and yellow lines
defining
the edges of the possible.

Maintaining a space,
the invisible bubble,
around the vehicle
hurtling down the road
and the keen observer
forever jailed
behind a blue-covered seat,
kept away from the wheel.

View from the Tayelet

A postcard picture
spread beneath our feet,
twilight lends the city
a holy pinkish glow
dotted with golden sparkles.

Joy fills the group
at the spot of a prayer
whispered fervently,
but after a solemn ceremony
one stands alone
eyes glassed by tears.

There is no one
to share the feelings
swirling through the air.

Coming home
to an empty house
makes the missing
ever more present.

Distorted Image

I'm a piece of trash.
Toss me around,
hold me in revision,
throw me out.

I'm less than zero.

Pretend I don't exist,
for my existence
means nothing to anybody.

I'm a ghost,
something to shun
and avoid at all costs.

Colorful Crime?

All the colors
have been captured,
kidnapped,
and put in boxes.

Someday soon
these hostages
will be abused,
broken,
worn down to nothing
all to the accompaniment
of giggles.

Goodbye

It's always so hard
to say goodbye,
so many things
remain unsaid,
unfinished.

Fragile Promises
of next time
shouted from the doorway
hang silently in the air,
ever more faint,
as the car disappears from sight;
but everyone knows,
even if next time comes,
it will never
be the same.

Aftertaste

I thought everything
was sweet as sugar,
forgetting
sugar always melts
when placed upon a tongue
and it is the sour lemon
that lingers.

Mothers/Children

Mothers must
think their children deaf
to talk about them
and when accused
deny it.

Perhaps it's only
that they lack sense,
believing it's their right
to say what they wish,
embarrassing the child
and pretending
nothing happened.

Wounds

Most wounds
will heal:
a cut or bruise
fades away,
stitches come out,
bones set.

Some wounds
leave scars
not always visible.

Part of me
has been left behind
in our old town.

Part of my heart
is broken
and feels
like it will never heal.

Waiting

Excitement
mingled with fear,
the countdown's begun.

I know what I'm doing
yet there's lots to be done.
10 days.... 9 days... 8 days....
It's really almost here.

My part,
I know it cold.
(O.k. I confess
inside lie doubts and fears.)

Why is this day so long?
Just a few more days
and it will be over too fast
swiftly becoming
a part of my past.

Fear

Cold
Spreading,
Eating its way
With long tendrils
Rising
From the pit of my stomach
Uncurling
Stretching up
Freezing
Chilling everything
Nothing
Left untouched
Paralyzing
Thoughts and body

Vanilla Confusion

I don't want the water
cascading over me
to wash away
the scent of vanilla
lingering still
from whispered darkness.

Yet I am bathed
in an uncertainty of desire:
my head
contemplating a step back,
my body
willing to rest on a plateau
until I know
more of the thoughts
dreams and memories
composing the body
scenting mine
with the feel of vanilla.

Eulogy for a Bridge Player

Dry bones grasped
stiff paper guises
of kings and queens
while a mind seeped in
past bids based on conventions.

With a sigh
the last king tumbled
onto starched white sheets
and her wrinkled neck arched
to kiss the pillow
one last time.

Smooth, sun-toasted fingers
shuffle the red-backed deck
and I am dealt
her twos and aces.

Blanket Cave Moments

I retreat
to where it's safe,
dark and warm
inside the cave
of myself.

There, I lick my wounds
and bar the entrance
so no one
can come in
to hurt me.

They tell me
to remember the good times
and ask if I had known
about the pain
engulfing me now
would I have given up
the moments of warm glow;
and I answer no
but wonder if maybe...
as I sink again
into the black of mourning
for the part of me
I'm trying to resuscitate.

Healing

Tonight, I walked alone,
under a canopy of stars,
smelling the crisp night air
and holding my head high.

The points of light
created pools on my path
and the frustrations
building for so long inside
melted like butter and chocolate
mingling on the stove.

I thought of you
with my head tossed back
to drink in the sky,
but for once
I didn't miss your presence.

I am what's important.
I.
Here,
in the serene
campus night,
I reign free
and I am strong.

Peaceful View

In a world
so full of noise and people
there is a spot
where you can see the earth
spread beneath your feet.

Perched up high,
the ground a distant green
punctuated with trees
while the blue skyline
reaches into infinity.

Blues and greens
mixing before my eyes
becoming one
with myself.